Teaching
and
Learning
with
YOUNG
CHILDREN

Teaching and Learning with YOUNG CHILDREN

A Manual for Workers in the Church

Grace B. Harger and Arline J. Ban

Illustrations by Linda Weller

Judson Press ® Valley Forge

TEACHING AND LEARNING WITH YOUNG CHILDREN

Copyright © 1979
Judson Press, Valley Forge, PA 19481

Library of Congress Cataloging in Publication Data
Harger, Grace B. and Ban, Arline J.
  Teaching and learning with young children.
  Bibliography: p. 60
  Includes index.
  1. Christian education of children. I. Title.
BV1475.2.H35   268'.432   78-26020
ISBN 0-8170-0803-9

The name JUDSON PRESS is registered as a trademark in the U.S. Patent Office.
Printed in the U.S.A. ⊕

Contents

Introduction

Welcome to a special group—workers with children in the church!

What challenged you to teach? Do you teach because you feel, "Well, it *is* my turn and someone has to do it!'"? Or do you teach because you can say, "I really like those children! It will be fun working with them!'"? Perhaps you remember people who helped you in your early growing years! Now you feel, "I can share my faith!" Whatever your reason, you know that working with children in the fellowship of the church is unique!

Working with children in the church is more than teaching a lesson! It is:
- sharing experiences with children,
  - taking time to discover children as persons,
    - observing and listening to the ways God moves in the lives of children.

You are invited to read this book to discover new ways to understand the children with whom you minister and new possibilities for creative teaching.

1

Who Are They?

Young children—
—are active. Pausing for brief moments to internalize (take in) all that is happening to them, they seem to learn "on the run."
—seek their level of need like water seeks its own level; will stop in the middle of active play to have someone hold them and read to them.
—have uneven, individual growth patterns. Sometimes it seems as if they grow faster than we can supply them with shoes and clothing. Then there will be periods of leveling off.
—"pick up" new words and phrases, new ways of seeing what is around them. A snowdrift becomes a magic mountain.
—are quick to sense changes in their environment.
—are full of questions.
—want to know about the tiny caterpillar on the sidewalk and the shadow that follows them as they run and jump.
—are dawdlers; yet it is their desire to explore which causes them to stop, look, listen, feel, and ask rather than just to pass by.

The more you live with the children in your church school nursery and kindergarten (ages three, four, and five), the more aware of their individual differences you will become. As you look at, listen to, and touch each child, you will begin to recognize the beauty, the potential, and the uniqueness of each one.

Children are engaged in developmental (growth) tasks which vary at the different age levels. They accomplish these tasks at their own pace. The clearest example of this is the development of walking and talking. Some children talk earlier than others; some walk earlier than others. This happens even with children within the same family. With this in mind, let's look at three-year-olds.

Introducing the Threes

I am me.
Look at me.
See what I can do?
I climbed to the top. Help me come down.
Let me put it on. Help me; my boot won't go on.
Look what I can do. I can crank the handle (of the ice-cream maker).
I can paint. See my orange picture.
Why does my caterpillar stay so still?
See me jump!
This is *my* song.
I can wash my hands myself—help me turn off the water.
Where is Mrs. Smith today? Why isn't she here?
I'm hungry.

As we look and listen to three-year-olds, we are aware that they are active; they need lots of space to run, jump, climb, and move around.

We discover that they use clay, paint, play with puzzles, and look at books all within a short time span. They are curious, but only briefly; then they go on to the next thing which catches their attention.

The threes are aware of the other children and teachers in their room, more than they appear to be, as they dart around investigating their environment.

Threes prefer the teacher on a one-to-one basis rather than in a group. Their need to be "center front" is very strong, and they sometimes find it difficult to share an adult with others.

A three-year-old will play with one or two other children. For example, he or she will play "going shopping" with another child as they both wheel carriages across the room. However, a three-year-old is aware of the total group and will ask about a missing member.

These same children, who as infants and toddlers developed a trusting attitude toward their world, now are expressing the need for autonomy. As infants and toddlers their needs were being met by loving, caring parents. They were snuggled, played with, and talked to; they felt the world to be a safe place to be and knew people as dependable and helpful. Soon, however, there emerges the need to use their new motor skills (running, jumping, climbing, putting on clothes, etc.). They want to use their new mental abilities which enable them to perform tasks for themselves. They want to buckle their own sandals (although it may take longer), pour their own orange juice, carry their overnight bag when visiting Grandma. As the three-year-olds are encouraged to do what they are capable of doing, they develop a sense of being able to control themselves and to a degree control what happens to them.

If these young children have everything done for them (because it is quicker) or if they are made fun of because the results are not up to adult standards, then they will doubt their own abilities. Later in life, they will experience difficulty in trusting their ability to sew, play the guitar, speak Spanish, or work a math problem. This is why we say to a three-year-old, "Let's get a paper towel and wipe up the orange juice. Then you can pour it again. Remember to stop at the blue line." Rather than, "Look what a mess! You didn't stop at the blue line!" This is also why we don't decide to save time by pouring the juice for them and depriving them of the right to try. Helping with their eating, dressing, and toileting seems such a little thing (just babysitting), but the way in which we do this makes a big difference in how children see themselves. When a child calls out, "See me! Look! I climbed up here all by myself," it is the expression of feeling of autonomy which Erik Erikson describes as a necessary stage in the healthy development of young children.[1]

How the Threes Grow in the Faith

Three-year-olds relate to God—
—when the persons who relate to them in loving, caring ways tell them, "God loves *you*. You are important. God cares about *you*."
—when adults share their feelings about God as the Creator of the natural wonders around them. As together adults and children enjoy rain, snow, birds, and animals.
—when they are made aware of God's gifts of plants to eat, trees for cool shade, and the warm sun to dry a swim suit.

Three-year-olds relate to Jesus—
—as the man who said, "Let the children come to me." The picture of Jesus and the children together is often a favorite. It is right on target with their feeling of *See Me!* They accept Jesus as someone who loves children because loving adults tell them so.
—because Christmas is Jesus' birthday and a time of celebration in their churches and families.

Three-year-olds relate to the Bible—
—as a special book, valued by the parents and teachers who value them.

The great biblical truths, love, forgiveness, and reconciliation, are best shared with children by teachers living out the gospel (Good

[1] Erik H. Erikson, *Childhood and Society* (New York: W. W. Norton & Company, Inc., 1963), pp. 251-254.

News) with them rather than by children memorizing the words of a Scripture verse.

Natalie (three years old) comes in on Sunday morning. Her body is shaking with dry sobs as her mother prepares to leave her at the door of the church school nursery. A teacher encourages the mother to stay for a few Sundays until Natalie feels more comfortable in her new surroundings and has begun to trust the persons there. On the Sunday morning when she can see her mother leave (confident that she will return) and eagerly participate in the nursery experience, then she will have experienced the Good News. Knowledge of words does not change behavior. Reaching the feelings of persons can bring about change.

Three-year-olds relate to the church—
—if the church is the place where children find persons they can trust.
—if persons will accept them on their not-so-good days as well as their best ones.
—if the church is a place where they can try out being responsible (in small ways) for themselves.
—if the church gives them a sense of belonging.
—if family and church friends reach out in loving ways, expressing their own good feelings about the church.

When three-year-olds are growing in the faith, they will experience and even express the joyous feeling of "This is my church!"

Meet the Fours and Fives

Four- and five-year-olds—
—can manage their bodies, ride a tricycle, cut with scissors, and defend their rights by hitting.
—can create their own activities.
—are making rapid progress in their use of language.
—have a vivid imagination. While riding a tricycle, they may say: "I'm riding my car to work. Give me some gas, please—thirty gallons. Here's my money—one dollar."
—are explorers/investigators. They may be heard to say: "How does this work?" or "Why does the cream turn to butter?"
—are physically active, yet can engage in quiet activities (listening to records, looking at books) for longer periods of time.
—tire easily and need a balance of active and quiet play.
—can share and take turns most of the time.
—can begin to help with the care of their room, helping to put the toys away, setting the table for "snack time."
—can recognize the feelings of others and relate them to their own.

Lucy said to Rachel (during rest time), "My head is tired." Rachel replied (in comforting tones), "Come to my house. My mother has baby aspirin. It will make your head feel good."

Timmy said to Tommy (a newcomer to church school), "Don't cry. Play with the clay. Make a snake. You'll feel better."

If four- and five-year-olds' attempts to initiate their activities are encouraged, they will feel that they can control, to a degree, what happens to them.

When their environment is always controlled
    ("Sit at this table. Cut out this picture."),
when their fantasies are derided
    ("You couldn't be a space man; you are not old enough."),
when their questions are passed over lightly
    ("I don't know why your dog died. Let's make a lamb using these cotton balls."),
they will feel a sense of guilt and inadequacy that is hard to overcome in later life.

When a teacher can say, in all honesty,
    "You really do know how to use the scissors";
    "Tell me about your picture. You used lovely colors";
    "You must really miss your dog. What did you and Sam do together that was fun?";
the children will have good feelings about their right to ask questions and to make decisions about what they do.

These are seemingly small happenings in the kindergarten room, but they make a big difference in how fours and fives see themselves.

How Fours and Fives Relate to God and Jesus

Four- and five-year-olds sense a loving and accepting God through the adults who share this feeling with them as they live together in the Christian community.

Matt and Mike were digging a hole. Matt asked, "Isn't this a *beautiful* hole?"

Mike answered, "It is only a little hole."

Matt, industriously digging away, affirmed, "It is a *beautiful* hole."

Mike offered a clincher, "God wouldn't think it was much of a hole."

Matt, continuing his digging, replied, *"My* God would say, 'Matt, that is a *beautiful* hole!'"

Four- and five-year-olds see Jesus as a loving person. They can truly celebrate Jesus' birthday. Birthdays and new babies are very much a part of their experience.

Rhonda (four years old) had a new baby brother. She was telling the Christmas story. She had the donkey clomping down the street, Mary singing "Rock-a-bye, Baby," and it ended with "Mary loved her new baby. She wrapped him in blue ribbons because he was a boy."

Four- and five-year-olds can know love to the extent that they are loved by parents and by others. They can understand the need for acceptance. They can understand, to a degree, the need to forgive and to be forgiven.

How Fours and Fives Relate to the Bible and to the Church

Four- and five-year-olds see the Bible as a special book, important to the adults around them. They pray as naturally as talking (if encouraged to do so). "Thank you, God, for all those gold buttons on our lawn." (Dandelions!)

Four- and five-year-olds talk about "my" church. They can feel themselves a part of the church community. The minister, teachers, and other church families are their good friends. Paul (four years old) said to his mother, in the supermarket, "There is my good friend, Mr. Brown! I see Jimmie's mother over there. They are at my church."

They can share with interest and concern for children in faraway places because they have grown up with television; people of other lands seem near and knowable.

They can sing with understanding:

> The church is not a building
> The church is not a steeple
> The church is not a resting place
> The church is people.
> CHORUS
> I am the church
> You are the church
> We are the church together
> All who follow Jesus
> All around the world
> We are church together.[2]

---

[2] From *The Avery and Marsh Songbook* by Richard K. Avery and Donald S. Marsh © 1972. Used by permission of Proclamation Productions, Inc., Port Jervis, NY 12771.

2

What Can We Do?

To teach young children is an invitation—
—to nurture feelings of mutual trust and acceptance: teacher to teacher, child to child, teacher to child.
—to encourage young children to discover who they are.
—to enable them to cope with their good, bad, happy, and sad feelings.
—to share God's love with them.
—to forgive them, enabling them to become forgiving persons.
—to provide for the use of their God-given sense of sight, sound, touch, taste, and smell as they reach out to the world around them.
—to help children recognize God at work in the world.
—to experience with them the joy of "becoming."

The nature of our ministry with young children is basically the same as that of the total ministry of the Christian church. Christians, both young and old, are confronted with the same questions: *Why am I here? Where am I going? Who is God? What gives meaning to my life? Who am I in the Christian community?*

The difference between the young and old lies in the ways in which they work out their answers to these questions. Adults and older children *work* at finding the answers to these basic concerns. Play is to be indulged in only after the completion of tasks. Young children, on the other hand, use *play* as a means of finding their answers.

Learning Through Play

For young children play is—
—their whole life.
—the opportunity to explore.
—the right to experiment.
—the chance to use materials in their own way (to create).

—the release from tensions.
—the exercise of large and small muscles.
—the development of coordination.
—the chance to achieve mastery of their own bodies.
—the medium for finding out about themselves and others.
—the opportunity to practice the skills of living as they see them.
—the occasion for trying out differing ways of behaving, discovering what works best as they relate to others.

What does it mean, then, when children are asked, "What did you learn in church school today?" and they reply, "We played."

Here is how one teacher saw it:

At the close of a sabbath morn, my little lads and lassies rushed through the portals to join their loved ones. A few came hurtling back for, alas, a forgotten painting, a cherished toy brought to share, O blessed thought, one more hug. Then silence fell and I was alone with myself.

As I wondered over the meaning of the morning, my Weaker Self took over and saith unto me, "What of importance tooketh place this day?" Did not Jamie spill the orange juice until the puddle spreadeth even unto the floor? Then my Better Self came to my rescue saying, "Was it not young Mark who brought forth the paper towels and with much sopping and mopping helpeth Jamie to a drier place where he might try again?"

Then my Weaker Self tempted me saying, "What didst thou teach this day?" There cometh to me the memory of the sobbing figure of Timmy, leaving his mother with gallant bravery, only to discover his defenses crumbling and his world a frightened place. Yea, I replied, I held a little one close and did feel the gradual lessening of tension and did rejoice as he slid away from me joining his companions in their play.

Then my Weaker Self mocked me, saying, "Is that all you teacheth?" I saw Jane painting at an easel. Surely hers was a wondrous mixture of paint. Truly she doth want to mix her colors, finding a lovely green from blue and yellow. Likewise, her purple arose from splashes of red and blue. And behold, we stood and looked together at this, her own creation, and it was good.

My Weaker Self was not satisfied and queried me further, "What didst thou teach this day?" I saw Amy pushing Rachel in a perambulator, and there was much conversation between them. Then my compassionate Amy telleth my uncertain, thumb-sucking Rachel, "You are my little girl and I loveth thee." Whereupon my unsure Rachel jumpeth up saying, "Now thou canst be the baby and I shall loveth thee."

Then there arose before me the closed eyes and folded hands of many children as tongues were loosed to speak to God so freely. Truly, God must rejoice in their much speaking and for their thanksgiving for juice, crackers that crumbleth into many pieces and all that has taken place in our church school that day.

Then my Better Self saith unto me, "Thou didst free thy little ones, to share with one another. Thou didst free some to bestow love upon another.

Thou didst allow thy children to experiment and didst rejoice with them as they findeth some answers. Thou didst release thy little ones to break bread together and didst join them in giving thanks to God. Go now in peace and prepare for next week. Thou knowest it has been good and thy children are filled with expectancy as they returneth to thee." For the children will reason earnestly among themselves saying, "Our teacher loveth us."

Grouping for Learning

Three-year-olds learn best in small groups of two or three. We space the activities within the room, therefore, in a way which will invite small numbers of children to be there at any given time.

Three-year-olds form their own groups informally and briefly, depending on their common interest. Picture the following:

two children painting at an easel,
three children playing at the water table,
one child making a puzzle,
a teacher and two children enjoying a book.

Every little while, the grouping changes as the children's interests move them from one area to another.

Three-year-olds want the teacher in a one-to-one relationship as often as possible; so teachers of this age group move from one area of the room to another, wherever they are needed. Sometimes they may be:

      listening to a single child,
      helping two or three children to play together more happily,
      singing with a small group.

For all groups of younger children, at least two teachers (men and women) are needed. This allows for one teacher to deal with an emergency, while the other cares for the group. For three-year-olds it is best, when possible, to have a teacher for every six children.

If you have a large number of fours and fives in your church, it is best to give each age group its own room. A group of twenty fours and fives can have a good experience, providing the space, leadership, and equipment are adequate. More than this number of young children in a room may cause confusion and fatigue for both teachers and children. When grouping four- and five-year-olds, keep in mind: Fours and fives—

—are active; therefore, we provide for active play.

—can stay with an activity for longer periods of time.

—need varied kinds of play and the right to make choices.

—still prefer small group experiences but are increasingly able to participate in larger groups for short periods of time. Their increased vocabulary and ability to share make it possible for them to contribute to a limited group experience.

—enjoy many of the types of play the threes engage in. In addition, they like to act out, experiment with musical instruments, move to music, and chant.

—want to experiment with scissors, paste, tape, and staplers.

—can enjoy stories (read or told) in a large group.

—can recognize the Bible as a book containing stories which teachers share with them.

As stated earlier, for all groups of young children in the church, provide at least two teachers (men and women). For fours and fives, a good ratio is a teacher for every seven children.

WHAT IF your church has only a few preschoolers?

• Threes, fours, and fives can be grouped together if the total number is small; the space is large enough to accommodate their activities; and there are enough teachers to meet their differing needs.

In this situation, there would be a special arrangement of the room so that the teacher working with the threes would use one part of the room. The teacher of the fours and fives would use the remaining section. Another alternative would be to use the kitchen, or an outdoor area, part of the time. This will be explained more fully in chapter 3.

The teacher for the threes would plan the schedule of activities for them. The teacher for the fours and fives would plan for them. Two teachers could be functioning in the same room (available for emergencies) but working with their own age group according to their needs.

Scheduling for Threes

Three-year-olds—
—need time to explore their environment.
—need an opportunity to use their large and small muscles.
—need some quiet times.
—need a "snack time."
—need an opportunity to help with the care of their room.
—need time for toileting, eating, and putting on outdoor clothing.
—enjoy variety but need to have enough sameness to give them a feeling of security.

One-Hour Session for Threes

Learning through play (40 minutes)
- welcoming children
- exploration time
- special activities dealing with the theme for the day
- cleanup

Routines (10 minutes)
- toileting
- washing hands
- giving thanks
- enjoying a snack

Preparing to leave (10 minutes)
- cleaning up from snack time
- getting on outdoor clothes
- saying good-bye to each child
- seeing that the children have their belongings to go home
- being sure the children are with persons responsible for taking them home.

Two-Hour Session for Threes

Learning through play (45 minutes)
- welcoming children
- exploration time
- special activities dealing with theme for the day

Routines (35 minutes)
- toileting
- washing hands
- giving thanks
- enjoying a snack
- a quiet time (maybe listening to some lullabies)

Directed activities (30 minutes)
- special activities related to the theme
- possible *short* field trip
- an occasional visitor
- playing outdoors (when possible)

Preparing to leave (10 minutes)
- cleanup
- dressing to go home
- collecting belongings (toys brought to share)
- giving a personal good-bye to each child
- being sure the children are with the persons responsible for taking them home.

Scheduling for Fours and Fives

When scheduling for fours and fives, remember that they need:
—time to explore.
—time for creative play.
—times to work alone now and then.
—opportunity to work in small groups.
—time to be quiet.
—a snack time.
—a chance to help care for their room.
—some "together time" when most of the children can listen to stories, dialogue, sing, move to music, etc.
—time to collect their belongings and prepare to go home.

One-Hour Session for Fours and Fives

Learning through creative play (25 minutes)
- welcoming children
- exploring the learning centers
- special activities dealing with the theme for the day
- cleanup

Together time (20 minutes)
- a time for songs, finger plays, stories (Bible and other), conversations, and prayer
- a time to give thanks
- snack time
- a time for conversation

Cleanup time (10 minutes)

Preparing to leave (5 minutes)
- giving children time to collect their belongings
- helping *where needed* to get into outdoor clothing

- being sure children are with the person responsible for taking them home
- giving a personal good-bye to each child.

The Bible and Young Children

Young children will value the Bible:
- if they see adults (whom they trust) using it.
- if we select the stories which are most like life as they know it (e.g., Jesus and the children, the birth of Jesus, a boy who shared his lunch, a girl who saved her baby brother).

The Bible provides us with a record of God's action among persons. Young children can recognize that stories about God and Jesus are found in the Bible and can remember and repeat short Bible verses appropriate to their lives and situation. They can recognize the Bible as a special book of our Christian faith. Its message of love, forgiveness, reconciliation, and self-worth will "become flesh" as the teachers "live out"—with them—the Good News.

Worship and Young Children

Young children can feel the presence of God as a momentary experience, often related to the wonders of the natural world. As children and adults hear the chirping of a cricket, see the colors of a seashell, or feel the softness of lamb's wool, it can be an awesome moment.

As children express pleasure and thanks for their daily happenings (e.g., ice cream to eat, the feeling of snow on their tongues, the smell of ginger cookies baking in the oven, their happy time at play), God seems very near.

Young children can occasionally be a part of the worship of the total church family. This experience will be most meaningful to them when preparation is made for their presence and when they are welcomed as participants rather than performers.

In his book *Will Our Children Have Faith?*, John Westerhoff describes several intergenerational worship experiences developed by clergy and lay people. These intergenerational worship services are examples of what can happen when persons in a congregation (pastor and people) discuss their needs and creatively explore ways to meet them.

If young children have an occasional experience in the church sanctuary, planned with them in mind, then at times of special celebrations (e.g., baptism, marriage, Christmas, Easter, memorial services) they will feel a sense of supportive belonging, as part of the total church community.

Christmas and Easter, high points of the Christian year, offer unique opportunities for young children to participate. Witnessing the lighting of the Advent candles will enable them to relate Christmas to a birthday celebration. The whole congregation could join with them in singing a Christmas carol they know. They could bring something they have made (place mats for the children's ward in a hospital) and leave it as their offering.

It is important to remember how difficult it is for young children to sit in a church pew or on their parents' laps for an hour or more. If your service of celebration is likely to be a long one, plan for the younger children to be present for only part of the time. Another alternative would be a short family service in which children are actively participating much of the time.

At Easter, the flowers may resemble a beautiful garden. Young children will enjoy sitting with their families, seeing and smelling the beauty around them. Again it is important to plan for their presence and to keep them in the service only as long as their growing muscles will allow. Five-year-olds will be able to sit longer than the threes and fours, of course.

Offerings and Young Children

Young children may offer a variety of things other than money. Threes sometimes find it hard to part with their coins or creations, but the fours and fives are able to understand some kinds of sharing. For example:

- They can bring canned goods for a community food locker. (They know what it feels like to be hungry.)
- They can make cards for the minister to take to sick people when he or she visits them. (They have been sick, too.)
- They can make a scrapbook for a children's ward in a hospital.
  (They may know someone who has been a patient in the hospital.)

Needless to say, their giving is most real and authentic when it is related to that which they know or have experienced.

3

How Can We Do It?

How Do We Organize for Threes?

Learning Centers. These are areas, in various parts of a room, which offer specific learning experiences. Here are some suggested learning centers for threes:

Building Center—offering opportunities to learn about construction and transportation (blocks become a church or a boat).

Home Living Center—offering opportunities to learn about such family life experiences as using the telephone, going shopping, eating, going to work, caring for the children, sweeping, cooking, and ironing.

See and Do Center—where children or teacher and children can look at books or play with games or puzzles related to the unit as well as other favorites.

Active Play Center—offering places to crawl into, climb up on, jump off of, rock in, etc.

Special Activities Center—an area which enables the children to "center in" on the theme for the day. This center changes from week to week and may include:
- a music center with records and wrist bells
- a place to touch, taste, and smell
- a place to visit with a church member and/or a new lamb
- a sand table
- a water table
- a quiet area
  (a place for quiet listening to records or just stretching out on a mat if they feel like it)

As stated earlier, the threes play alone or with one or two other children. Learning centers give them the opportunity to move about, choosing the center which fits their need at any given moment.

WHAT IF you have a few threes, fours, and fives and one teacher? Be sure there is someone close by who could deal with an emergency. However, one teacher could
- offer two or three learning centers each Sunday, changing them from time to time.
- offer another adult an invitation to come in for a special visit (e.g., a teenager with a guitar, an adult to tell about some special rocks or seashells, a nurse to talk about health and hospitals, a parent with a special skill or special interest). These visitors would share in a one-to-one or small group situation.

Routines. Snack time can be enjoyable around a small table with three or four friends; this is better than having all the children at one large table.

It is important for the nursery church-school rooms to be located as close as possible to toilets and sinks. If toilets and sinks are too high for young children, provide sturdy boxes for them to stand upon.

Preparation for Leaving. The threes can locate and remove their clothes from hooks the right height. They may need help locating a purse, a mitten, or a lost rubber. It is wise to use clip clothespins to keep each child's clothing in one place. Be sure the children have any artwork they want to take with them and/or any books or toys which they brought with them. One church-school nursery group uses large, brown paper grocery bags (decorated by parents at a parents' meeting) as a special storage place for each of the children's belongings. A personal good-bye should be given to each child.

How Do We Organize for Fours and Fives?

Learning Centers. These offer the same kinds of specific learning experiences for fours and fives as they do for threes. The fours and fives expand their use of the space and materials.
- They have an increased vocabulary.
- They are more capable of sustained (longer) play.
- They interact more with one another.

Here are some suggested learning centers for fours and fives:

Home Living Center—offering opportunities to dramatize the following family situations: going to work (father or mother or both), returning home, using the telephone, visiting, entertaining, cooking, cleaning, caring for the children.

Building Center—where children can use large blocks and masonite cylinders to construct familiar objects: an organ, a train, a car, or a boat.

See and Do Center—here fours and fives can use their abilities to look at books more carefully, noticing story sequence and detail; some are able to read. At times, much conversation between children will happen here, as they share a book, a puzzle, or a game. For the shy child, it is a place to meet the familiar and not to have to cope with other persons at first. Therefore, it is strategic to place this center near the entrance.

Art Center—fours and fives are saying, "Let me try." This center offers them the opportunity to experiment, to create. It also allows for the release of feelings as they mix, brush, drip, and combine colors.

Active Play Center—an area for jumping, hopping, and climbing. In this center, fours and fives can arrange some of their own play (if the equipment permits this). A balance beam becomes a bridge. They find it easier to take turns than the threes did and are generally more independent in their play.

Special Activities Center—a place for materials for special projects related to the theme for the morning. It changes from time to time, as the theme develops. It might be an area for making a mural, a conversation with a visitor, or blowing bubbles and finding the beautiful colors within them.

A Quiet Area—a place to listen to records, to relax. It is important for fours and fives to discover that quiet times are nice times, too. If the session is two hours, this area is especially important.

Routines. Snack time can be one of the more relaxed, quieter times as four or five children and a teacher sit at small tables to enjoy a cool drink or celebrate a birthday. Fours and fives can help to set the table (a napkin and a cup), pass the crackers, or pour the juice. It is a time for conversation and giving thanks for the morning together.

Offer the opportunity for toileting and washing hands before eating. Encourage the use of soap and warm water.

Preparation for Leaving. Children can remove their own wraps from the hooks and put them on with minimal help. They can then go to their storage space and collect all items or messages to go home. Each of the children should be given a personal good-bye.

Organizing for Music and Art

As we organize for learning, let's give some special thought to music and art.

Music is a part of the nursery church school because children are there and music is as natural to them as breathing. They sing as they play (with or without words) and beat out rhythms with fingers and toes. They clap, turn, jump, and twirl to music. They listen to a recording, a guitar, or an autoharp. They can relax listening to soothing music.

With the threes the teacher seems to be doing all the singing. Later parents will report that their child is singing new songs at home.

Three-year-olds—

—enjoy rhythmic, short melodies with repetition of words.

—like songs using their names.

—like songs about each other.

—like songs about the seasons.

—like songs about the holidays.

—like action songs.

In the nursery church school, music is a part of many activities (e.g., painting to music, swinging to music, cleaning up while singing).*

Music with fours and fives is also spontaneous and natural. It can be used when taking a walk, painting, skipping, playing a game, or cleaning up. Most fours and fives also enjoy total group experiences with music. The fives especially like active singing games.

Four- and five-year-olds—

—like songs about themselves.

—like songs about family.

—like songs about growing.

—like songs about the seasons.

—like songs about helping.

—like songs about the church.

—like songs about the holiday.

—like songs about birds and animals.

Their expanded vocabulary allows for a greater variety of songs, and they are able to enjoy longer songs at this age.*

An important aspect of music in relation to young children is its place on Sunday morning. It is not a formal learning experience in which some children succeed and others fail. Rather, it should be a sharing of thoughts and feelings.

Art, like music, should also be experienced as natural and spontaneous. When we place limits on children's art—when we insist that it all be alike and that it follow our directions—we deny them the right to be themselves. If we provide them with necessary tools and materials, allow them the freedom to experiment, and permit them to develop in their individual styles and at their own pace, we are encouraging their "becoming."

*Consult "Resources," page 60.

Many young children are content with the process (e.g., finger painting, string painting, making a collage) and ignore the finished product. Other children cherish every snip of paper they cut, every painting they do. Parents need help in receiving the artwork presented to them. If they can be helped to understand that the *process* is often more important than the *product,* they can accept the work with whatever explanation the child offers.

"Here is my paper, I used yellow."

"This is a dragon on the way to the beach."

Nor will parents who understand the importance of the process feel the need to have a piece of artwork given to them every Sunday.

Sometimes a child will be too busy with other play to go to the Art Center.

Sometimes, a child's collage is a part of a total collage, hung in the room.

The Art Center, in the nursery or kindergarten church school, is a place where the experience can be the child's very own.

In organizing for this learning, the teacher's role is:

- to provide a variety of materials (a few at a time).
- to protect children's clothing.
- to protect the area in which children are working so that they do not have to be overly concerned about spilling and dripping.
- to encourage and support the children in their efforts to experiment with different materials.
- to allow for the individual development of skills.

4

What Do We Need?

The Room for Threes

The room needs to have:
- 35 square feet of floor space per child. Young children need space (clean, light, and airy). For young children, open space is more important than furniture.
- cheerful primary colors (red, yellow, blue) rather than pastels.
- a clean, warm rug on the floor.

Equipment and Materials for Threes (a suggested list)*

books that are mostly pictures (make use of local library)
a Bible
wooden puzzles (6–8 pieces)
pictures placed at children's eye level
record player, variety of records—to move to; to hear a story; to rest by
a water table
a sand table
a tunnel to crawl through
a climbing dome
a rocking boat
a child-size stove, sink, refrigerator
unbreakable dishes, pots and pans
dolls (male and female, representing different races)
doll beds, doll carriage
telephones
modeling clay

cookie cutters, Popsicle sticks, rolling pins
sturdy wooden trucks, planes, boats
set of large blocks
for the sand table: muffin tins, cake pans, sieves, Jell-O molds
for the water table: eggbeater, bubble pipe, squeeze bottles, plastic cups, funnels, varied lengths of rubber tubing
paste
paint, long-handled brushes
easel, tray, and cups for paint
scraps for collage: yarn, cloth, lace, ribbon, buttons
two small worktables
resting mats (washable rugs) if there is room
a rocking chair (adult size)

smocks (pieces of plastic tablecloth). Cut a piece just wide enough to cover a child and twice a child's height, with a hole in the middle for the head to go through. This makes an easy coverall for a child to use at the painting center or water table.

paper: large pieces of newsprint; various textures, shades, and colors of paper; shelf paper (glazed); wall paper

*Consult "Resources," p. 60, for equipment catalogs.

> **WHAT IF** you have limited space and few children?
> • Select from the list and change from time to time. Perhaps a small nursery group and a small kindergarten group could exchange periodically.
> **WHAT IF** you have a limited budget?
> • Perhaps adults in the church could make suggested items. Some recommended equipment might be donated by families in the church.

The Room for Fours and Fives

The room needs:
• space—25–35 square feet of floor space per child, if possible. Again open space is more important than furniture.
• a clean, warm rug on the floor.
• light and air.
• colorful, clean walls with space for hanging pictures, children's artwork.

Equipment and Materials for Fours and Fives

Bible
pictures
record player
rhythm instruments
child-size stove, refrigerator, sink
table and four chairs
dolls (male and female, different races)
doll bed
doll carriage
dishes, pots, and pans
brooms, mop, ironing board
dress-up clothes
stethoscope
hats
water table

sand table
magnifying glass
puzzles (10—18 pieces)
salt and flour clay
smocks (for painting and water play)
large crayons
blunt-tipped scissors that cut
paste, Scotch tape, stapler and staples
collage material: string, yarn, buttons, trim
climbing apparatus
big blocks
resting mats (small rugs)
storage shelves

books that are easy to read, with many pictures (longer story sequence than for threes)
paper: large newsprint, manila drawing paper, colored construction paper, glazed shelf paper, wallpaper

Space and equipment enable young children—
—to discover who they are in relation to others.
—to explore space.

—to use their bodies in various ways.
—to think.
—to try out behavior.
—to make choices.
—to assume responsibility for their own behavior.
At best the space, large or small, will be arranged:

- to encourage children's curiosity.
- to continue their sense of adventure.
- to nourish their belief in themselves.

Space and equipment are important, but the most important factor in the learning situation is the teacher. The power of love to lessen children's feelings of rejection, to relieve their hates and urges to destroy, to remove their feelings of inadequacy—in short, to redeem—is the power of God at work. The teacher "becomes the Word and dwells among them." Therefore, be glad and rejoice that you are called to minister to children in God's name.

5

Our Ministry with Children

Our ministry is guiding children in their Christian growth. It is a ministry that can happen at different times and in many ways. Sometimes it takes place in the church school class, on camping retreats, on visits to shut-ins, during family events, while working together on projects or creative activities, in experiences of discovery, or while sharing in play. The possibilities for ministry are endless. However it happens, our ministry with children focuses on the nurturing of the *child's awareness of and response to God.*

Let's look at some things we can do to help us be more effective in this ministry.

Affirm each child as a person of worth. This is a good place to begin! The message of our ministry is that God loves all people. God is accepting, forgiving, and loving, and God wants us to grow and respond to that love. A child is better able to understand God's love when he or she experiences love and acceptance from others.

Before we can affirm children in honest ways, we need to know each child well. No two children are alike! Think about the boys and girls with whom you work. List the ways each child in your group is different from the others. Some of the differences you might be aware of are:

- how they are growing.
- abilities they have.
- their willingness to try new things.
- what they understand to be good behavior.
- how they get along with persons their own age.
- how they feel about themselves.

How do we affirm a child? Sometimes affirmation is spoken, such as: "That was good thinking, John." "I'm glad you asked that question!" "Keep using your imagination, Beth. It is good to find different ways of doing things." "Good work!" "How well you two work together!" Each child has something we can encourage from time to time.

There are many unspoken ways to affirm children, such as:
- helping two children settle an argument.
- showing tender care in caring for any physical needs.
- helping an older child find information about a question that seems important.
- giving a hug when it is needed (or even when it is not).

- taking time to listen to a child tell about "wild imaginings," that might make little sense to you.

In whatever way we show affirmation, the child needs to feel we are saying, "You are all right! You are important to me!"

It is easy to affirm children who are happy and always seem to do the right thing. But how does one respond to children who are difficult? Jill throws spitballs whenever she can. Bill withdraws from the class and only wants to stare out of the window. Marge is a disturbance in any group activity and distracts other children. Steve is a tease.

Children need to know that they are accepted and loved even

though what they do is rejected. It is best to separate what the child *does* from what the child *is*. We can do this by avoiding "put downs" or "personal threats." Rather than saying, "Jane, you always cause trouble," or "You can't come back if you do that again!" speak to the child in a way that says you trust him or her to correct the action. For example, "Let's see how we can have a better time."

A child who disturbs others or withdraws from the group has a reason for doing so. Think about why the child is acting in a disturbing way. Is it a need for attention? Is it boredom? Does the child need someone else in the group with whom to work or play? Help the child gain attention in positive ways. For example, find a way for an older child to share his or her special abilities in the learning activities. Enlist the help of a younger child in caring for plants in the room. Show your trust in the child's ability to help and cooperate in a situation. See "Resources" in the back of the book for reading material related to discipline problems.

Children will be more open to being aware of God and responding to God when they experience self-worth in the Christian community.

Create an environment which demonstrates warmth, trust, and care. The environment is people, the feelings in a situation, the room, the activities that happen. The environment is all that surrounds and influences a person. Children are influenced most by the persons who care for them. The place where children gather can also give out good feelings.

A well-lighted, comfortable room helps to build positive attitudes toward the Christian community. On entering a room, a child immediately senses whether he or she wants to be there. When there are things to touch and look at, displays of things children have done, and a promise of activities that will take place, a child wants to get involved. On the other hand, a child does not have much interest if the room is immaculate, sterile, and looks as if nothing exciting could ever happen there. In an inviting environment, whether it is in a space filled with church pews or in someone's living room, the good news of God's love can be felt and experienced before and while it is talked about.

Guide toward an understanding of the Christian faith. This has to do with the message we have to share. It centers in the Bible as a record of God's action among persons in the past, God's revelation in Jesus Christ, and God's action through the Holy Spirit and in the Christian community today.

Through the years we want children to gain a knowledge of the events and people of the Bible. As they grow older, so may their understanding of God's message in the Bible deepen and become a resource for their living. Sharing the message also means guiding a child's growth toward a commitment to the sovereignty of Jesus Christ. The child is able at different stages of development to discover meaning in the life and teachings of Jesus that will help in relationships and decision making. Learning about God's activity through the people of God in the past and within the Christian community today is important.

To grow in knowing about and experiencing the Christian faith is a lifelong task. This is expressed in the following statement.

> *The objective of the church's educational ministry is that all persons be aware of God* through God's self-disclosure, especially God's redeeming love as revealed in Jesus Christ, and, enabled by the Holy Spirit, *respond in faith and love;* that as new persons in Christ they may *know* who they are and what their human situation means, *grow* as children of God rooted in the Christian community, *live* in obedience to the will of God in every relationship, *fulfill* their common vocation in the world, and *abide* in the Christian hope [1] (author's italics).

This objective has special importance to our ministry with children. In one sense, it spells out the basic goal of Christian education. Yet, there are no "pat answers"; there is no single way of acting or thinking that must be learned. It does not assume that by a particular age or grade a child will know certain information and facts. Nor does it assume that a person's awareness of God or a particular response to God will happen at any one time in life. The objective has an openness that allows for varying degrees in awareness of God and response to God at each stage of a person's growth.

For the child, the difference will be in terms of individual development, readiness, and experience.

Becky, for example, watches her cat give birth to kittens and then care for them fastidiously. As a result of watching her pet, Becky begins to think about what life is and how animals and humans know how to care for themselves. At this point of her interest, Becky's understanding of God as Creator and Provider may begin to take shape. Becky has an experience which makes her ready to ask questions and understand meaning.

On the other hand, there is Jimmy who is the same age as Becky

---

[1] *Foundations for Curriculum* (Valley Forge: Board of Educational Ministries, American Baptist Churches, U.S.A., 1966), p. 13.

and in her class at school. Jimmy knows the church as the place he is told what he "ought" to do or "ought not to do." He is afraid of being rejected at church. Jimmy's ideas of God are shaped by his experiences there. Jimmy has difficulty becoming aware of a loving God and responding to God with gratitude and love.

The objective of the church's educational ministry has an interesting characteristic. It assumes growth. Each of us from the youngest child to the oldest adult may continue to grow in any of the points mentioned in the objective. The degree of our awareness of God and response to God will differ depending on our maturity and experience. This is the experience of growing and becoming in the Christian faith.

A Shared Ministry

Your teaching task is one part of a larger ministry with children. This nurturing ministry is shared with the entire congregation. Many congregations make a commitment when parents dedicate their children in an act of worship. At this time a promise is made to support the parents and to provide various ways to help the child to grow in Christian love.

Christian congregations are responding to the needs of children in a variety of practical and creative ways. Churches are providing nursery schools, kindergarten classes, day-care centers for working parents, and programs for children in need of special education. Some after-school programs offer opportunities in creative expression through art, music, and drama. Other churches provide space and leadership for community clubs, libraries, and athletic programs. Many church school classes are moving to an afternoon or evening time when it is more convenient for children and adult workers to gather. Camping, weekend retreats, or backpacking trips for older children have become favorite ways to involve adult leaders, young people, and older children informally in sharing the Christian faith. There are many possibilities in a nurturing ministry.

Not only are events and programs planned specifically for children; but also, whenever possible, children are involved with adults in meaningful ways in the total life of the congregation. Such participation is where children come to know Christianity as a way of life to be lived.

As children share with others in worship, fun times, fellowship events, in the sharing-caring ways people help each other, they will come to experience the church as a community of faith through whom God works today.

What You Can Do

Have you ever wondered, "Why am I here? What is the purpose? What will I teach? How will I do it?" In our ministry with children it is not only *what* we teach, but also *the child* whom we teach that is important.

As a teacher your role will be that of a guide and a resource person. You are not expected to be an expert who has all the information to give to children. You will invite the children to learn by providing an opportunity, stimulating their interest, providing resources and guidance, sharing your faith. You will learn along with them and from them! You will help children to think about what they have learned and what meaning it has for their lives.

Look again at the statement of objective on page 37. You will notice that it not only gives direction to our ministry with children, but also we may use it as a check on what we are doing. It can help us evaluate what is happening with children. We can ask ourselves: *What difference does this session or activity make to the child in moving along the lifetime objective of being aware of God? How does it help the child grow toward responding to God?*

You Are Not Alone

Considering our ministry with children may leave you with the feeling "How can I do it all?" There are others who share this responsibility.

Usually an elected group cares for the total program of Christian education within a local church. Their responsibility is to provide leadership, space for activities, and resource materials as well as to make decisions about children's activities. They will count on you to let them know when you have needs in any of these areas. Perhaps you would like to have training in teaching skills. Or you may think there is a need for a particular activity, such as a children's choir. This committee will make the decision on these activities and help to facilitate them.

The pastor also shares this responsibility for ministry with children. There are many ways a pastor can help: talking over your teaching situation with you, coming to observe what you are doing, helping you in teaching an idea, being one of the teaching team for a couple of sessions, directing you to resources to help in your teaching. This person may welcome an opportunity to work with you.

Other persons in the church share your task. Those responsible for "outreach" or contacting unchurched people may visit families of children who do not belong to the church. Committees working with mission activities can include the children in planning and carrying out specific mission projects. Adult church school classes may provide transportation, counselors for camping experiences, or they may share in service projects. Parents may form a study group to discuss the themes you are working with in order to find ways to reinforce learnings in the family. Parents might also take turns as "teaching aides" when needed.

The planned and spontaneous ways of ministering with children ultimately depend on the work of the Holy Spirit. The objective of Christian education describes the work of the Holy Spirit as an "enabling force." As the spirit of the child is moved by the Holy Spirit, he or she may respond in faith and enter into fellowship with God in Christ.

The Holy Spirit will enable you as a teacher to have the power, strength, and love to provide an open, inviting teaching-learning situation in your ministry with children.

6

Children and Learning

How Children Learn in the Church

Children learn in the church essentially the same way they learn in any other place. Let us look at five important considerations in the process of learning.

Children are able to learn when they are ready—physically, emotionally, socially, intellectually. We do not expect a nursery child to do the same kind of playing or thinking that we expect of a kindergarten child or a first grader. We need to be aware of the characteristics of growth stages, so that we can help children learn at their own point of readiness.

For example, think about Mary, a nursery child. When she is expected to hold a Bible and repeat a memory verse in church school, she may learn that the book is heavy, has small black things, and strange pictures on the page. Mary may also learn that the book is very important to the teacher. The verse she repeats makes the teacher happy. Mary has not yet developed in her ability to understand the meaning of the verse. Mary's language development is limited. She can repeat what someone else tells her to, but that does not mean that she understands the meaning. Mary thinks in intuitive and pre-logical rather than abstract ways. She may be able to say through imitation, "Jesus loves me," or "God loves me." She better understands "Mommy loves baby " as she sees her mother care for the baby. Plan for all children, nursery age as well as older children, to learn in ways that fit their abilities.

Each child is different. Some have abilities and experiences that others do not have. Susan and Cliff are in the fifth grade. Susan has moved with her family many times and makes friends easily. Susan has little difficulty taking part in a group discussion about *how* Jesus' teachings can apply to relationships in her school life. Cliff is quiet, tends to be withdrawn from the group, and is artistic. Cliff is uncomfortable discussing Jesus' teachings with others. On the other hand, he is able to think through meaning as he illustrates a comic strip. Individual differences make it important for us to understand each child in terms of that child's own unique characteristics and readiness to learn.

Children want to learn when they have a need to learn or an experience that stimulates them to learn.

Take Cory as an example. Cory tries again and again to ride his brother's two-wheel bike, but his legs are not long enough to reach the pedals. He does not yet have the coordination or balance to ride the bicycle. When Cory is physically able to learn this skill, he will do so quickly. Then he will have the ability to match his desire to learn.

A child may be mature enough to learn a particular skill, but unless he or she sees a reason for it, there will not be as much interest to learn. A group of sixth graders visited a shut-in as a part of a study on the mission of the church. They talked with her about what they did in school, their pets and hobbies, and some of their activities in church school. In turn, she shared with them memories of early days when the town was only a village and the church consisted of two families meeting in a home. It was an exciting visit for both the children and

the shut-in. Afterwards, as they talked about the visit, an idea grew for a project to care for shut-ins in their church and neighborhood.

Children learn best when they are involved in the learning process. Learning is not like a spectator sport. The learner has to take part in it to make it happen. It is not enough to sit by and watch a well-prepared teacher do his or her own thing. Let's look at some ways to involve children in their learning.

Usually, you set goals to clarify your own purpose for teaching. Share these goals with the children. They want to know what they are going to do and why. "In this session (or in the next few weeks), we are going to be thinking about. . . ."

Better still, involve the children in setting the goals. The extent to which children can share in planning depends on their age and ability to do so. We can involve children by finding out what they already know and what their questions are. It may take some time to talk with the children and listen to their ideas. When learners make plans for themselves and the group, care needs to be taken to be sure they are realistic. Think through together such questions as: *Where can we find out information? Whom do we know who could help us? How much time do we have to do this? What activities could we do to help us understand and express the meaning?*

Learners become interested when they are a part of the decision making and carrying out of the plans. Children may also be involved through exploring, finding answers to their questions, working out an idea through activities, and evaluating. The sixth graders described earlier became involved in many ways. They made a visit in which they shared their own interests and activities; they evaluated the visit and then planned and carried out a project.

Involving the children in what happens encourages them to develop self-confidence and to understand their own abilities.

Children learn best when they can relate what they are learning to their own lives.

The team of teachers in one kindergarten class felt satisfied with the completion of a unit around the theme "Friendship." They had used several activities, including dictating stories and illustrating them, dramatizing Bible stories with puppets, sharing with senior citizen friends in the church. They were especially glad to observe Ellen, who was shy and withdrawn, beginning to accept another child as a friend. One day some of the children were building in a learning center. Ellen accidently knocked down the building project. The children were angry and there was some cruel name calling. Ellen seemed to shrink away. The teachers looked at each other in despair. Their looks said,

"What have we been teaching all these weeks?" In a careful way they talked over with the children what had happened. Allowing feelings to be expressed, the teachers showed they understood how disappointed the children felt. They also helped them understand how Ellen felt and how the name calling hurt her.

After the session, the teachers evaluated what had happened. These are some of their findings:

1. They had assumed the children were friends and did not need to grow in relating to each other. The emphasis in the activities had been on friendship with others outside the group.

2. Learning is more than covering the material in a book.

3. Learning takes a long time and a lot of patience. Repetition of an idea is necessary for it to become a part of a person's life.

4. Learning happens when children apply what they talk about and do to their own real-life situations.

Children learn in a variety of ways. Children do have different learning abilities. They learn at different rates of speed and in different ways.

Amy, a fourth grader, is first to say, "What do I do now?" She finishes her art work first. Tom has not developed the ability to cut well. He will be last to finish his work on the project. Amy cannot read well, but Tom reads several grade levels ahead of his own grade. A variety of approaches to teaching will allow Amy and Tom to learn in their own personal ways and give each child a successful feeling about learning.

A few of the many approaches to help children learn are through seeing—pictures, maps, films, chalkboards; hearing—stories, music, records, people sharing experiences, singing, reading; doing—research activities, creative activities (art, drama, role play), discussing, taking field trips, carrying out service activities.

Learning is a personal thing. Each person takes from a situation that which she or he needs or wants and is able to take. In planning for our ministry with children, we need to know each child well. Then we plan opportunities in which that child has the freedom to learn about God's love and respond to that love.

How Children Grow in the Christian Faith

Growing in the Christian faith is a gradual process that continues through life. It is personal. It is based on a child's unique growth patterns and experiences. As we try to understand how the child grows physically, socially, emotionally, and intellectually, we need to apply the same understanding to the child's religious growth. One

way to categorize development in the Christian faith is in terms of
. . . feeling
. . . thinking
. . . acting out.
Growing in the Christian faith cannot be separated from what the child experiences and how the child perceives or understands those experiences.

Feeling

Let us take Mike as an example. Mike comes from outside the Christian community. He is a bright fifth grader who is functioning far below his ability in public school. Mike has had a stormy childhood. He lives with his mother and third stepfather together with other children from three marriages. The father and mother have never had stable employment. They live marginally in a crowded two-room house. Mike's mother is quick to criticize him and punish him physically. Mike has never known security, loving care, or trust. One day he attended a neighborhood church with a friend. He did not understand the sermon, but he did feel the warmth and acceptance of the adults. These feelings led him to return. Mike thinks about God in terms of fear and punishment; these ideas have grown out of his experiences. From what Mike picks up from television and other sources, he associates Jesus and religion with magic.

Mike's Christian growth hinges on his gaining feelings of trust and stability in his world. Before he can move on to thinking about God as love, he needs to be able to count on others. He will need to experience love that is forgiving when he fails. The first step in faith-growth is the feeling of trust, love, and acceptance. This is a need of the youngest baby in the nursery to the oldest child.

The feeling that one is a person of worth is also important. Each child is in the process of testing out who he or she is in the world. The baby asserts herself or himself by announcing a need by crying. Older children test their strength by climbing trees or rebelling against their parents. They are in search of who they are. They need to feel their own identity apart from the family and as a part of their own age group. The church family can help children to grow in self-confidence and self-acceptance. As children are enabled to relate to teachers and other boys and girls, to explore, to use their own initiative and make choices, they have a chance to develop feelings of self-worth. When children are growing in these feelings, they are also growing in their ability to respond to God through Christ.

When a child experiences trust and acceptance in the church

family, he or she may feel that these are people who love. Before children are able to know what the Christian faith is all about, they may feel they are members of a church family. As they share in the worship and informal gatherings, they may feel that these are people who stand for something. These positive feelings about the people of God become associated with the Christian faith. Positive feelings will lead children to grow on the "thinking level" in the Christian faith.

Thinking

"Thinking" about the faith begins early in life when the smallest child asks questions. The questions are prompted by what the child sees, such as a picture of Jesus with the children, or the passing of the offering plate in the worship service, or family members saying grace before meals.

The ability of children to "think" about religion coincides with their intellectual development. At each stage of life, each child has a special way of looking at the world and explaining it in terms of his or her "own set of eyes." The youngest children understand everything in relation to what is happening to them. ("I like chocolate pudding!" "Thank you, God, for chocolate pudding!") Elementary children tend to think in concrete, literal ways. They can understand Jesus who was a child like them or as a man who really lived. Older elementary children are only beginning to think in abstract, symbolic ways about religion. As children grow in ability to think, meanings of the Christian faith will be easier to grasp.

Ideas of the Christian faith are easier to understand when the person "thinks" about them as they are related to life experience. Take the Bible, for example. Some older children are able to memorize Psalm 23. The language of this poem is beautiful and symbolic. When children study Psalm 23 from the point of view of how a Palestinian shepherd lived, they may be able to understand the danger, the feelings of aloneness, thankfulness, and dependence on God that a shepherd might feel. As the children discuss the psalm in relation to the times when they themselves feel danger, aloneness, thankfulness, and a need to depend on others and God, the meaning will be clearer. Only after "thinking" about the meaning of the passage will the truth be learned.

Church school teachers sometimes share too much, too soon with children. They sometimes feel an urgency to tell children more about the Christian faith than they have a capacity to understand. A good test of what you are expecting of children on the "thinking" level is whether you can translate the ideas into the language and experience of the age of the children with whom you are working. Children grow in their ability to understand the faith as they grow intellectually.

Acting Out

Children operate on an "acting" level in Christian growth when they determine their own behavior. This happens when a child moves from imitating others or doing what is expected by others to a point of "acting" because he or she believes it is right to do. A kindergartner may share a puzzle with a new child out of genuine desire to be a friend to the newcomer. That's growth! An older child may resist a temptation to cheat out of conviction rather than a sense of "ought" or "fear." That's acting out Christian values.

Jesus set the example in teaching by asking many questions to make his followers "think" about how they would "act out" biblical meanings in their lives. The decision for "acting out" the Christian faith rests with an individual child. The action will be stimulated by how that child "feels" and "thinks" about his or her own life circumstances and how he or she wants to respond to God.

Children with Special Needs

Children with special needs may have physical, mental, and/or emotional characteristics that differ from those of other children. How can you plan in the church school for Tom, whose hearing is impaired; or Susie, who is blind; or Chris, who is mentally retarded; or Jim, whose emotional problems are the cause for disruption Sunday after Sunday; or Peter, the bright, gifted child? Tom, Susie, Chris, Jim, Peter—each has a right and a need to know God's love and the acceptance of the Christian community.

Hearing Impairment

Hearing impairment may range from mild to complete deafness. Speech and language disabilities often accompany the hearing loss. Learning through "seeing" will be the key to understanding. Visual aids, as well as lip reading and signing, will help to communicate ideas.

Use simple language and talk directly to a child with hearing difficulties. A short, direct statement is best when explaining new words, a story, or an idea in a visual presentation. Be sure your face is in full view of the child. It is not necessary to shout or to exaggerate movements of the mouth.

In one church school, a young adult who knew sign language was asked to be a part of the teaching team. She not only interpreted ideas for a deaf child, but also she taught a small group of children to read and use sign language.

Blind or Partially Blind

Blind or partially blind children develop their other senses to compensate for the lack of vision. In the church school, as in other situations, they learn best by experiencing an idea or concept through feeling, hearing, tasting, and smelling. For use with these children, choose materials for art activities such as wood, cloth, and clay, which are good for touching and feeling. Blind children can take part in discussions or dramatizations by using puppets. It is also helpful for them to listen to recordings or tapes. Older children or youth could make tapes of the material the other children will be reading. For children who have learned to read Braille, Bibles in Braille are available through the American Bible Society.

Mental Disabilities

Children with mental disabilities are often not able to socialize with children of their chronological age. They cannot grasp the ideas that come easily to others. They have short attention spans. They frequently are moving a foot or an arm and are easily distracted. Each child is different.

There are several ways we can help the child with mental disabilities have an easier time within a class of normal students. It is important to provide a structure for the child so he or she knows what is expected and what the limits are. Changes in routines are disturbing to these children. It is best to have one adult who works with a child on a one-to-one basis. The adult may help the child know what is expected of her or him and provide a firm, consistent control for the child. Plan to use activities that are less demanding and on a grade level where the child is functioning. Find out from the parents what the child can do best.

Emotional Difficulties

Jim enters the room with a scream and starts knocking over chairs. Because he is an emotionally disturbed child, the causes and effects of his behavior are many. His learning ability is not usually different from the others, but he will function well only when he discovers friendship and trust in the teacher and the group. Such a child needs one teacher with whom to relate in a special way. This teacher's task is to love and accept the child no matter what he or she does. On days when the child is having a "rough time," this adult needs to give sole attention in a quiet spot. Here the two may talk or work quietly on an activity. This child requires much assurance, affection, affirmation, and firmness.

The Gifted Child

Peter's ability may be considered a handicap as he often faces the misunderstanding of teachers and others in his peer group. As a gifted child, Peter's mental age is much higher than his chronological age. He learns faster, remembers more, and tends to think more deeply about what he learns. Often in the middle of a discussion, Peter takes off on a tangential interest—which makes sense to him but to no one else in the group.

Gifted children may seem shy, obnoxious, or antisocial. They need to be encouraged to think for themselves. A common characteristic of a gifted child is to conform in order to be accepted, rather than give an idea that is different. The gifted child's abilities can be put to work to enrich learning activities in the church school. A younger child may tell about a story he or she has read or share a hobby. An older child may be given some research to do. Care needs to be taken in guiding gifted children to respect others who do not think or learn in the same way as they do. Contrary to what we might think, gifted children need to find self-esteem.

The "special" child needs to have a satisfying feeling of belonging and contributing to the group. A teacher's attitude sets the tone for how other children respond to a "special child." When you show acceptance, respect, expectation, and patience for the person who needs extra consideration, the boys and girls are apt to follow your example. Avoid placing the child in circumstances where the "difference" is obvious. At such times, it is easy for the others to make fun of or feel superior to the child. It may be necessary to find a time—when the special child is not present—to discuss the differences openly and find ways the children may show their understanding. Children need to know how painful teasing can be. Then they may begin to help each other grow.

Additional leadership is necessary as we include children with special needs in the regular activities of the church. Team teaching, parent volunteers, or assistance from young people can facilitate a teaching-learning situation in which each child has a chance to know God's love.

Children Are Teachers, Too!

Children who are free to bring who they are and what they know to a group share in the teaching-learning experience. In effect, they, too, are teachers.

Children have a natural curiosity and sense of adventure. Teachers may be led by children to explore questions they ask or try their suggestions for a "new way" to do an activity.

Children also have an uncanny way of zeroing right through a complex problem to the simple truth of the matter. Adults will struggle with how to help children relate the meaning of a Bible story to their lives, and then, behold, a child will do the task in a very clear, direct way. Listening to children becomes important as teacher and learner discover meaning together.

Children today have a lot of information. They sometimes do not know what to do with all they know. One teacher thought as he looked over his class, "You know more than I will ever know, but I think I can help you understand what you know."

Teachers who are open to children will learn from them, take what they share, use it, and grow in their own understanding of the Christian faith.

7

Teachers and Teaching

The Role of the Teacher
—as an enabler of learning

Your role as teacher is primarily that of inviting children to share with you in learning. The teacher is responsible for preparing for a session with appropriate objectives for a group of children. The teacher is not *the* authority or power figure. In our ministry with children we like to think of the teacher as an "enabler"—one who helps children to do their own learning. The role of the teacher-enabler is:

- to stimulate the interest of the children.
- to be a resource person who suggests meaningful activities for learning.
- to be a guide in helping children to think through the meaning of biblical material, play experiences, and relationships.
- to help create a community feeling among the children so that they might feel free to express themselves, ask questions, and take the initiative in finding out about the Christian faith.

—as a model in terms of attitudes and behavior

What do children learn from what the teacher says and does? Children first size up a teacher from a self-centered view: "Does he like me?" "Does she think my ideas are good?" A teacher's own expression of love, understanding, and forgiveness of children is readily caught. The teacher's first task is to communicate God's love.

Children next see the teacher as one who is phony or real. They quickly sense when a person is not what he or she pretends to be. Children enjoy a real person for a teacher—one who is a friend and shows interest in them. Yes, they can even respect a person who gets angry and seems a bit bored at times. But how they do enjoy sharing humor and fun with teachers! The teacher who is big enough to admit "I blew it!" "I made a mistake!" is helping children know it's okay to make mistakes. Mistakes can be corrected and forgiven in oneself and in others.

A teacher's attitude may be: "This is the way it is. I know!" or "I'm here because I need to learn and grow with you!" The second attitude helps children to know that one can continue to learn all through life and that God is active in the experience of learning. Children learn many things in quiet, unexpected ways. The teacher is an important model for the growing child.

—as a communicator of values

Children learn values from the important "key" people in their lives. At a young age they become aware that people differ in what they think is "right" and "wrong." A little child is told "No!" while she or he watches another child do the same thing and get away with it.

Television viewing exposes children to a variety of life-styles and values in our pluralistic society. Older children do wonder: *What is right? What is wrong? How can I make a decision?*

You as a teacher communicate values that are important in the Christian community. One way to teach values is to demonstrate them through the learning activities. Children are learning values when they are planning, sharing, looking for meaning, and doing things for others. Such activities can say that human life has value, that persons are different, have rights, and deserve respect.

The Christian church "lives out" the values it stands for in the activities of the church fellowship. You can help the boys and girls understand the reason for the activities and the values they represent. Better still, find ways for them to participate in the activities. Children may see the fellowship, caring, and supporting, believing that life is a gift from God, believing that life is worth living, believing that there is hope for a better life, and worshiping God through prayer and rituals.

Sharing your own convictions is important: "This is what I believe. . . ." "From my experience. . . ." "The way I see things now. . . ." "This is why. . . ." Sharing one's point of view must not mean *imposing* values on children. Share in such a way as to encourage learners to make their own commitment to Christian values.

The Team—or Working Alone!

When teaching with a team, each person shares in guiding the total learning experience in each session. Each team member is a teacher. Each one is aware of what might happen at every point of the session from beginning to end. The team together is ready to give guidance in activities as the session moves along.

A team prepares by planning, studying, praying, and evaluating together. Each person is encouraged to use his or her special abilities

in teaching. Planning involves deciding who will be responsible for the different activities. A team teacher may be assigned a small group activity or a learning center. That person will then prepare for the activity by gathering necessary materials and information. Some teaching teams find it wise to choose a lead teacher for each session. This "key" person is responsible for getting the session started, making transitions, and guiding the children when they are together in a group.

Many teachers find the team approach makes it easier for them to relate to children on a one-to-one basis. Particularly in a large group, children with special needs can be reached when there is more than one teacher. It is also easier to encourage children in their relationships with one another. Because of the possibilities for a variety of groupings and activities, there is often a more informal atmosphere with team teaching. Team teachers also model, through their working together, a relationship based on respect and Christian love.

Teaching alone also works! The teacher working alone will adapt plans and materials to suit the size of the group. The lone teacher will also think realistically about the abilities he or she has to carry out a plan.

A teacher is never alone, however. Children and teacher can be a team. Very young children can become helpers in putting things away. As children grow older, they may share in planning, setting up the interest centers, finding resources, and carrying out separate group projects. It helps to make a chart listing the responsibilities when tasks are shared with children. Allow children to choose what they would like to do. Provide for frequent changes. Older children often work well in small groups or committees. They may be able to plan what they will do and how they will do it with just a little guidance from the teacher. One of the children can be chosen as chairperson. He or she will get the group organized and working on its task, and then report the progress being made by the group.

Whether teaching alone or as a team, it is more satisfying to share the responsibility with others.

A Relationship with the Home

The home is a major influence in a child's life. In our fast-changing world there are a variety of home situations: a traditional nuclear family, a single parent family, an extended family with relatives and/or friends, a group home or institution, a foster home, or a flexible group with people moving in and out.

What children experience in their homes also varies. They may share with the family in talking over problems and in working together. They may seldom see their parents or other members of the family. They may come from a one-child family or they may have brothers and/or sisters. They may suffer physical and/or emotional abuse. They may go on trips which widen their experience or have other privileges which help them to know about the world.

The child's experience in the home affects how he or she learns in the church. The teacher needs to know about each child's home situation.

Keep in Touch

1. Make a personal call in the home to get acquainted with family members.
2. Make phone calls to let those at home know you are interested in them and in the child's Christian growth.
3. Send letters home to give information about learning activities, special projects, family events, parent meetings.
4. When a child is absent, follow up with any of the ways mentioned

above. Alert the pastor immediately if you hear about a family member who has a serious illness or when there is a crisis.

5. Find ways to encourage parents or other adults in the family to guide the child's Christian growth.

6. Send home the parent pieces from the curriculum you are using.

7. Plan study groups in areas such as parenting, children and Christian growth, and Bible study.

8. Enlist family members in learning activities when you need extra help, when they might assist in a particular project, and when they have information or skills to share which fit into your theme of study.

Continuing to Grow

Teaching children is time consuming and demanding. A teacher soon senses the need to grow as a Christian and to renew a sense of perspective. Growth for adults, as for children, is a continuing process. Growing is personal. Growing is enabled by sharing experiences with others.

We who work with children need from time to time to stop and look at ourselves and ask: *What have I learned? What do I want to become? What growth goals would be good for me right now?* Take some time to think about your own needs for growth. Jot down a list of your ideas. Choose one or two realistic goals.

Teachers become learners when they study child development, learn how to plan and guide learning activities more effectively, study the Bible, talk over theological ideas with others, or participate in denominational or ecumenical teacher-training events.

Teachers, like children, learn through questioning, searching, discovering and working with new ideas. Teachers, like children, are learners!

8

Teachers and Planning

Planning is the key to effective teaching. Planning provides a framework and direction for teaching. A teacher with a plan used as a guide can move from it when the situation demands a change.

Planning a Session

Let's look at some practical steps to help you plan a session.

Step 1. Know the direction

Curriculum materials provide this direction for most of us. Skim through the material to get a sweeping overview of the entire course. Statements of purpose are provided in the curriculum. You will notice that sessions are organized into units or clusters. Each unit or cluster has a specific purpose which fits into the overall theme. If you do not use curriculum materials, think through the theme around which you will plan activities.

Step 2. Bring together information

- *About the children*

What are their needs? Interests? Resources?

What kind of experiences do they have which will help them find a personal meaning in this session? Think about individuals. What happened in the last session? What questions were asked that still need to be answered? What activity was left unfinished?

- *About the teachers*

What skills, strengths, and experiences do you have that will enrich this session? What resources do the other teachers have?

- *About the teaching situation*

What kind of space do you have? Is there enough room for the learning activities? What kind of equipment and materials do you have with which to work?

Step 3. Check your information

Look at the information you have gathered. What does it tell you? What does it mean? How do you need to adapt the suggestions to fit the needs and resources of the children and the teachers? Is it possible to find additional space in another room or in a hall to carry out some of the activities?

Step 4. State an objective for the session

An objective is a statement of what a child may learn in a session, rather than what the teacher will do. For example: "The child will know God as one who seeks change in people, and who can be counted on to forgive and love him or her." Many teachers find it helpful to set down *specific* objectives for each session. These are written in terms of what the child will be able to know or do by the end of a session. Here are examples of specific objectives for one fifth grade class:

Find the biblical account of Jeremiah's speech at the temple.
Describe what God expected of people.
Define the word "covenant" in its biblical meaning.
Identify ways people live according to God's covenant.

Objectives help to guide the selection and sequence of activities that go into a session plan.

Step 5. Make a plan

1. Think through learning activities you will use. Are they realistic as you consider the children, the time, the room, and the equipment? How will they help the children apply meaning to their lives?

2. Plan when you will do each activity. Look at the Sample Session Planning Sheet. What activities can be used at the beginning of the session to interest the children? What activities are best when all children are together, work in small groups, or work alone? How will you involve children in evaluating? How can you close a session?

3. Consider the details. Who will be responsible for each activity? How long will it take? Where will you do it? What materials will be needed?

Step 6. Carry out the plan

Be flexible enough to allow for children's ideas and spontaneous kinds of learnings.

Sample Session Planning Sheet

Unit Purpose

Session Objective(s)

What We Will Do	Time Needed	Who Is Responsible	Materials Needed
Room Arrangement (What will make it attractive, practical for activities, interesting?)			
As Children Arrive (The session begins with the arrival of the first child.)			
Session Development Group together Small groups Interest groups (Use of play, conversation, discussion, creative activities, music, audiovisuals.)			
Closing Moments (A time for sharing, summarizing, evaluating, worship, planning ahead.)			
Evaluating			

Step 7. Evaluation

Teachers and children alike need to evaluate. Children may evaluate at the end of a session by talking over: *What did we like best? What did we learn? What questions do we have? What suggestions do we have?* At the end of a unit, evaluation may involve summarizing what was learned in the previous sessions.

The teacher's evaluation will focus on objectives chosen for the session. What happened to indicate the extent to which objectives were reached?

Careful planning insures a good feeling for the teacher and children. Teachers may be more realistic in what they expect. Children are quick to respond when they sense there is a purpose for their gathering and there are exciting things to do.

Using Resources in Planning

Curriculum resources are graded to enable the best teaching-learning experience. The materials often include books for children, resource books with session plans for teachers, and other aids, such as pictures, maps, charts. They are planned for a broad audience and so require local adaptation. Curriculum resources may be ordered from denominational publishing houses.

People have rich resources to share. Look around in your own church and community for people who have traveled, do community social work, or have experience in church missions. It is more exciting to hear persons tell about their own experiences than to read about them. People who have special gifts and hobbies might help with special projects. Senior citizens might tell about your church's history. Their presence will also help children appreciate another generation. You could also invite a church leader to join your class in order to help the children learn about how the church and its people work.

There are many printed resources which help to enrich learning activities. Some of these are: different Bible translations, Bible atlases, Bible dictionaries, maps, posters, and children's books about typical life situations.

Audiovisuals—filmstrips, films, slides, records, tapes, flat pictures—help to clarify meaning and add interest in a session. Curriculum materials often suggest specific audiovisuals to use in a session. School district audiovisual libraries and public libraries are good sources for materials to use with children. Other possible sources include denominational offices, ecumenical centers, and neighboring churches.

Selecting Resource Materials

The first thing to look for in choosing supplementary materials is whether they are designed to help the children you teach to learn and grow in the Christian faith. Do the materials take into consideration how children learn at that age level? Are the materials attractive? Would they be appealing from a child's point of view? Are the pictures colorful and free from too much detail or symbolism? Will they last under hard use by children? When choosing books for children, look carefully at the readability level. Are they written for the reading level and experience of the children with whom you are working? Is the type large enough?

When selecting curriculum materials for elementary children, ascertain how the child will use the material. Does it encourage thinking, the use of creative activities, and does it offer a variety of suggestions so the child has a choice? When choosing teacher's resources, see how many different ways to teach are suggested. What kind of biblical and theological help is provided? What kinds of directions or practical help are included?

Adapting Resources

Not all curriculum resources will fit every person or situation. They are intended as guides. One group of children may work more slowly or faster than another group. With older children there may be a need to expand plans for a session into several sessions to include more activity so that interviews, field trips, and panel discussions may enhance the learning. The amount of time for a session will determine how much of the material it is possible to use. It is more important to remain flexible to meet the needs of the boys and girls than to cover all of the material suggested for each session.

Caring for the Details

Accurate records are essential for our ministry with children. Complete information about every child should be recorded (home address, phone, parents, church affiliation, age, grade in school, name of school, etc.)

This basic information can be obtained when the child is first enrolled. It needs to become a part of a permanent record. Teachers will then make changes in the record as it is necessary. When children come to church alone, someone needs to make contact with the home.

Each teacher will want to keep a separate record which includes, in addition to the basic information, personal notes regarding the child's interests, abilities, and problems. This information may help the teacher to understand the child better. It is for private use only.

Individual attendance records are also important. It is not enough to count heads for the total church school attendance. When a child is absent, we will want to find out the reason. This will help us to be aware of illness or other problems. Showing our concern and interest is important to our ministry with the whole child.

The manner of offering gifts of money differs with each situation. In many churches children have envelopes to place in the church class offering or in the congregational worship service. Children in other churches drop coins in a basket on the table in their room. Whatever your pattern, help the children know what they are doing and why. Children too young to understand the concept of "offering" may think they have to pay for being in the church. Guide the children in understanding how the money will be used to do the work of the church. It is good to have a special time to call attention to the offering by singing or saying a prayer of thanks. In this way, the act of offering may come to mean responding to God with thanksgiving.

Now, It Is up to YOU!

The ideas in this book have been shared to help you in your ministry. In no way are these ideas the last word. There is so much more to discover about children, about ourselves, and about the ways we can be more effective in our ministry. A structure for teaching has not been set for you to follow. The ingredients have been suggested. What happens in your own teaching-learning situation depends on what you and others do.

Glance again through these chapters. With pencil in hand, let the ideas stimulate you to think and dream. What might you do? Let your imaginings lead you to set some long-range goals toward which to work. You may discover there are some ideas you can work with right away! We hope that your study and imaginings will make clear to you the ways your ministry is unique!

Yes, you have a special task! It is up to you to find ways to allow each child with whom you work the freedom to grow in awareness of God and in response to God.

Resources

For Use with Young Children

Recordings

Birds, Beasts, Bugs and Little Fishes, by Pete Seeger. Available from Folkway Scholastic Records, 906 Sylvan Ave., Englewood Cliffs, NJ 07632.

You'll Sing a Song and I'll Sing a Song, by Ella Jenkins. Available from Folkway Scholastic Records, 906 Sylvan Ave., Englewood Cliffs, NJ 07632.

Play Your Instrument and Make a Pretty Sound, by Ella Jenkins. Available from Folkway Scholastic Records, 906 Sylvan Ave., Englewood Cliffs, NJ 07632.

Ideas, Thoughts and Feelings, by Hap Palmer. Available from Educational Activities, Inc., Freeport, NY 11520.

Pretend, by Hap Palmer. Available from Educational Activities, Inc., Freeport, NY 11520.

Song Books and Recordings

Come Sing with Me. Available from Judson Book Stores: Valley Forge, PA 19481; 670 E. Butterfield Rd., Lombard, IL 60148; 816 Figueroa St., Los Angeles, CA; Green Lake, WI 54941.

The Fireside Book of Children's Songs, compiled by Marie Winn and Allan Miller. Available from Simon and Shuster, Rockefeller Center, 630 Fifth Avenue, New York, NY 10020.

Equipment Catalogs

Community Playthings. Rifton, NY 12471.
The Formative Years. Clifton, CT 06413.
The Growing Years. Childcraft, 20 Kilmer Road, Edison, NJ 08817.

On Working with Young Children

Church Options for Day Care. Philadelphia: Geneva Press, 1973. Packet of pamphlets offering guidance for churches considering day-care programs.

Hemphill, Martha Locke, *Weekday Ministry with Young Children.* Valley Forge: Judson Press, 1973. A manual for the church weekday nursery school.

Jenkins, Gladys Gardner, et al., *These Are Your Children.* Glenview, Ill: Scott, Foresman and Company, 1966. Describes and illustrates children's growth and development.

Kessler, Diane Cooksey, *Parents and the Experts.* Valley Forge: Judson Press, 1974. Help for parents in judging the varied child-guidance approaches.

Kindergarten Portfolio. Association of Childhood Education International, 3615 Wisconsin Avenue, NW, Washington, DC 20016. Twelve leaflets of interest to workers with kindergarten children.

Newbury, Josephine, *Church Kindergarten Resource Book,* revised edition. Atlanta: John Knox Press, 1970. Planning and program ideas.

Newbury, Josephine, *More Kindergarten Resources.* Atlanta: John Knox Press, 1974. More planning and program ideas.

Nursery School Portfolio. Association of Childhood Education International, 3615 Wisconsin Avenue, NW, Washington, DC 20016. Twelve leaflets of interest to workers with nursery children.

Smith, Leona J., *Guiding the Character Development of the Preschool Child.* New York: Association Press, 1968. Principles and methods for parents and teachers in guiding the child's growth.

Wangner, Florence. E., *Resource Portfolio of Nursery Education Handbooks.* Valley Forge: Board of Educational Ministries, ABC, U.S.A., 1968. Ten handbooks on such subjects as storytelling, room arrangements, and children, ages two to four.

Widber, Mildred C., and Ritenour, Scott T., *Focus: Building for Christian Education.* Philadelphia: United Church Press, 1969. Deals with room arrangements and equipment for children.

General

Christian Education and Hearing Impaired Children: A Few Suggestions for Work with Eight to Twelve-Year Olds. New York: Education for Christian Life and Mission, National Council of Churches, Room 708, 476 Riverside Drive, New York, NY 10027. A packet of materials.

Duckert, Mary, *Help! I'm a Sunday School Teacher.* Philadelphia: The Westminster Press, 1969. A practical how-to-do-it approach to teaching in the church school.

Duska, Ronald, and Whelan, Mariellen, *Moral Development: A Guide to Piaget and Kohlberg.* New York: Paulist Press, 1975. Explains stages in the moral development of children in a readable and understandable way.

Geyer, Nancy B., and Noll, Shirley, *Session Planning for Church School Teachers.* Valley Forge: Judson Press, 1971. Moves the reader through a step-by-step approach to session planning.

Gleason, John J., Jr., *Growing up to God: Eight Steps in Religious Development.* Nashville: Abingdon Press, 1975. Describes theological issues he thinks are dealt with as persons grow up.

Isham, Linda, *On Behalf of Children.* Valley Forge: Judson Press, 1975. A perspective on the needs and resources of children which may shape our ministry with children.

Laymon, Charles M., ed., *Interpreter's One-Volume Commentary on the Bible.* Nashville, Abingdon Press, 1971. Provides maps, photographs, drawings, commentary, and help on chronology.

Martin, C. Lewis, and Travis, John T., *Exceptional Children: A Special Ministry.* Valley Forge: Judson Press, 1968. Practical suggestions for teaching methods to use with handicapped persons.

Rood, Wayne, R., *On Nurturing Christians.* Nashville: Abingdon Press, 1972. Helps teachers reflect on their faith and ways their faith can be effectively shared.

Westerhoff, III, John H., *Will Our Children Have Faith?* New York: The Seabury Press, Inc., 1976. Chapter 4 offers a look at how persons grow in the Christian faith.

Index